One-Minute
PRAYERS®
to PRAY *for*
YOUR KIDS

HOPE LYDA AND MICHELLE LIND

HARVEST HOUSE PUBLISHERS
EUGENE, OREGON

Cover design by Bryce Williamson
Cover photo © Dari Dombrovskaya / Gettyimages
Interior design by KUHN Design Group

For bulk, special sales, or ministry purchases, please call 1 (800) 547-8979. Email: Customerservice@hhpbooks.com

One-Minute Prayers® to Pray for Your Kids
Copyright © 2022 by Hope Lyda and Michelle Lind
Published by Harvest House Publishers
Eugene, Oregon 97408
www.harvesthousepublishers.com

ISBN 978-0-7369-7815-6 (Hardcover)
ISBN 978-0-7369-7816-3 (eBook)

Printed in China

22 23 24 25 26 27 28 29 30 / RDS / 10 9 8 7 6 5 4 3 2 1

CONTENTS

Love the LORD your God with all your heart and with all your soul and with all your strength. These commandments that I give you today are to be upon your hearts. Impress them on your children. Talk about them when you sit at home and when you walk along the road, when you lie down and when you get up.

DEUTERONOMY 6:5-7

IDENTITY

MAY MY CHILD ALWAYS KNOW
WHO THEY ARE IN YOU AND
THEIR VALUE AS YOUR CHILD.

PURPOSEFULLY CREATED

Before I formed you in the womb I knew you,
before you were born I set you
apart; I appointed you.
JEREMIAH 1:5

Lord, I will never forget the first moment I realized I carried my child within me. I knew even then that this child was a gift. I will never lose sight of the blessing you created and the miracle of this gift, but I know that the love in my heart cannot even begin to compare with the love in your heart.

You created them with such detail. Each piece of DNA. Each strand of hair. Each bone in their body. Every aspect of their personality. These are displays of your perfect craftsmanship. Lord, fill my child with an understanding of just how amazing this is! They are a perfectly unique representation of your image. May my child feel the depth of your love and understand how valuable they are to you.

THE INTIMACY OF HIS PRESENCE

---

*Don't you know that you yourselves are God's
temple and that God's Spirit dwells in your midst?*
1 CORINTHIANS 3:16

Heavenly Father, open my child's eyes, today and every day of their life here on earth, to understand that you have taken up residence within them. Lord, may they know that as your child, they do not walk through life alone. No. They are set apart. You are not a distant God to your children. You are always with them.

Lord, thank you for the intimacy of your presence. I pray that my child will recognize your Holy Spirit dwelling within them. Constantly remind them that they are connected to you. They are yours. And when they became yours, you took up residence in their heart. O Lord, may they know how deeply you cherish them. A child of the King. A temple of the Most High God.

CHOSEN

You are a chosen people, a royal priesthood,
a holy nation, God's special possession, that you
may declare the praises of him who called you
out of darkness into his wonderful light.
1 PETER 2:9

Lord, you place a call upon the lives of mankind. You determine each soul that is chosen, each life that will dwell with you in eternity. Lord, I ask you to bring clarity into my child's mind. May there be no doubt of your affection. May there be no doubt of their value and worth to you.

You have chosen. You have anointed. You, O Lord, have given your creation purpose and meaning. Father, I am asking you to help my child stand confidently in your light, in close proximity to you. Lord, I know my child is not perfect. May they never be content with a life apart from you—a life of darkness. Instead, Lord, please draw them near to you. Help them to understand how beloved they are to you.

PERFECTLY CONSTRUCTED

———

*You created my inmost being; you knit me
together in my mother's womb. I praise you
because I am fearfully and wonderfully made;
your works are wonderful, I know that full well.*
PSALM 139:13-14

You value my child in ways they may never know this side of eternity. You purposefully and perfectly constructed each detail of who they are. What you deem beautiful isn't always what we desire most for ourselves. We criticize your handiwork and desire to change it.

Instead of trying to fit the world's mold of beauty, may my child seek those things that are beautiful to you. Humility. Kindness. A loving heart. Talents used for your honor and glory. Obedience. Graciousness. A giving nature. A passion for you. Increase the value of these traits in my child's mind, Lord. Clothe them in that which is beautiful to you.

LOVED AND VALUED

See what great love the Father has lavished on us,
that we should be called children of God!
And that is what we are!
1 JOHN 3:1

Lavish your love upon my child, Lord. Drench them in your goodness. Overwhelm their spirit with the awareness of your presence. Remove any doubt of their value and worth to you. Instead, fill them with the confidence of their sonship to you. This is your child. Loved and cherished by the King of kings and Lord of lords. Ground them in the knowledge of this identity. Set apart, chosen, and dearly loved.

GOD IS YOUR CONSTANT

Neither height nor depth,
nor anything else in all creation,
will be able to separate us from the love of God
that is in Christ Jesus our Lord.
ROMANS 8:39

Circumstances change. Relationships come and go. The good in life runs simultaneously with the bad. These things hold true.

Yet you, Lord God, are greater than these things. Your love weathers the storm of circumstance. Your faithfulness will not fade like human relationships do. Your goodness and mercy far exceed the bad things life can bring. Lord, help my child to find their refuge in you in the midst of it all. Bring about a lifelong awareness of your incredible love for them. A love that will not fade. A love that knows no limits. A love that is not based on merit. Undeserved, unlimited, and perfect love.

PURPOSE

MAY MY CHILD KNOW AND EMBRACE
WHAT THEY ARE CREATED FOR.

REVEAL YOUR PLAN

For we are God's handiwork,
created in Christ Jesus to do good works,
which God prepared in advance for us to do.
EPHESIANS 2:10

You designed my child. You have given them gifts, talents, and abilities. Some have already been revealed. Some are still known only to you. You have created my child to play a specific role in this world.

Open my child's eyes to your purpose and plan for them. Reveal to them, Lord, how you desire them to use what you have given them for your glory and to fulfill what you have prepared for them. All that they are is yours. Lead them step-by-step to do the work you have ordained them to do, that they may live in faith and obedience to you and that you may be glorified by their good works.

PLANS TO PROSPER

---

*"For I know the plans I have for you," declares
the L*ORD*, "plans to prosper you and not to harm
you, plans to give you hope and a future."*
JEREMIAH 29:11

Nothing can thwart the plans of the Most High. Your plans are to prosper my child and to be their bulwark of hope and the guarantor of their future with you.

Father, align my child's heart to yours. Direct them throughout this life into actions of righteousness. Mold my child's heart so you are their first priority. Lead them in the right direction—away from sin and temptation—so that you may shower your blessings upon them. Be the foundation upon which their life is built. As long as they live, may they strive to obtain the prize of dwelling in your presence.

EACH DAY IS PLANNED

Your eyes saw my unformed body;
all the days ordained for me were written in
your book before one of them came to be.
PSALM 139:16

There is comfort in knowing that you have already ordained each day of my child's life. You have already seen every day, every moment. You are aware of every circumstance or situation. You are familiar with the entire time my child is here on earth, from conception to the grave.

Do what only you can do, Lord. Carry my child each day in your loving and capable hands. Bring them through each mountaintop experience and each valley with a firm grip on them. Each day is an invitation for my child to know you in a deeper way. Each day is an opportunity to grow, to gain understanding, and to accomplish your purpose.

A PLAN AND A PROMISE

He who began a good work in you
will carry it on to completion until
the day of Christ Jesus.
PHILIPPIANS 1:6

There is only so much I know to do, Lord, only so much I know to ask on behalf of my child. Yet I know that you have a plan and promise that I can pass on to my child. Heavenly Father, remind them that they can confidently rest in the truth that you will finish in them that which you began from the moment of their creation. You will carry it to completion.

O Lord, every time my child feels discouraged or inadequate or questions why you created them as you did, remind them of this truth: You will use them to complete a good work for you. Others may not see it, and my child may not always feel it, but I claim it as a promise for my child.

ALWAYS THANKFUL

Rejoice always, pray continually,
give thanks in all circumstances;
for this is God's will for you in Christ Jesus.
1 THESSALONIANS 5:16-18

You desire a grateful heart, Lord. It is easy to lose sight of the blessings you have given and to complain about our unmet wants and disappointing circumstances.

Lord, help my child to always be thankful for your provision. Open their eyes to your goodness. Even when life doesn't go as they plan or hope, please help them maintain a heart of gratitude toward you. You are worthy of praise, and there is much to praise you for, even in the hard times. May praising you, being in fellowship with you through prayer, and giving you thanks in the midst of life's circumstances become deeply ingrained in my child's spirit and habits.

AN AWARENESS OF YOUR ANOINTING

*Whatever you do, whether in word or deed,
do it all in the name of the Lord Jesus,
giving thanks to God the Father through him.*
COLOSSIANS 3:17

As my child grows, I ask you to help them be aware of your hand upon them. I don't want my child to go through life wondering if they are making a difference for you in their work lives or their relationships. I want my child to know that you have a plan and purpose for them and that they are living in it.

Reveal to my child that you have anointed them to play a specific role in this world. Help them understand what you have perfectly designed them to do, and guide them in that direction so they can find the purpose and satisfaction that comes from cooperating with you. Save them from wasting their life, and assure them that they are glorifying and honoring you.

DISCERNMENT

MAY MY CHILD NOT BE FOOLED OR
WOOED BY THE WORLD, CULTURAL
INFLUENCES, OR ANY DECEIVER.

STRENGTH TO STAND IN TRUTH

---

*...so that your faith might not rest on
human wisdom, but on God's power.*
1 CORINTHIANS 2:5

The world does not recognize your power, Almighty Father. But of course, your power knows no limits and has no bounds. Impress upon my child—deep within their core—a faith that will not be twisted or manipulated by anything that would deny your goodness, strength, power, and holiness.

Instead, Lord, expose our culture's narrative for what it is, and declare the truth of your character to my child. As they grow in this discernment, Father, help them to find strength to stand in the truth even when the world goes against it. Be their strong tower. Be their protector. Be their fortress. Be the rock upon which they stand.

DEEPLY ROOTED TRUTH

---

*Dear friends, do not believe every spirit, but
test the spirits to see whether they are from God,
because many false prophets have
gone out into the world.*

1 JOHN 4:1

Lord, protect my child's mind from the lies and deception that are continuously presented to them as truth. Pour out upon them the gift of discernment so that they are aware of anything that disguises itself as true but actually pulls them away from living in obedience to you.

May your Word be so deeply rooted in their heart and mind that they are able to easily detect the lies that contradict it. Bring about the clarity that only you can provide to those who seek to bring honor to your name.

DISCERNMENT AGAINST DECEPTION

I am your servant; give me discernment
that I may understand your statutes.
Psalm 119:125

O Lord, protect my child from deception. Save them from empty promises that fame, power, and money claim to offer. Empower them to overcome the temptation to sin. You have promised that there is no temptation beyond what they can bear and that you will always provide a way out of it. Lord, help my child to let your promises take root in their heart, mind, and soul.

Instead of sin, help my child to know and value what brings blessing and abundant life. Help them to desire it…even crave it! As my child studies your Word, help them understand and apply what they read. Let it not be merely printed words on paper; rather, let it be as you designed it to be—the living Word in their life.

TAKING THOUGHTS CAPTIVE

---

*See to it that no one takes you captive through
hollow and deceptive philosophy, which depends on
human tradition and the elemental spiritual
forces of this world rather than on Christ.*

COLOSSIANS 2:8

A war is being waged on our children, Lord. I know you see it. I can only imagine how deeply it grieves your heart. You revealed your love for children when Jesus invited them to come and spend time with him. Jesus made it clear that God's kingdom belongs to those who are like children.

I lift my child to you out of concern and love. Please save my child from falling for man's philosophies and from being subtly deceived into believing anything that contradicts Christ. I am asking for protection over my child's heart and mind. Empower them to take their thoughts captive to you. Help them to recognize distortions and lies, and inspire them to cling to the truth.

AWARENESS OF YOU

This is my prayer; that your love may abound
more and more in knowledge and depth of insight,
so that you may be able to discern what is best and
may be pure and blameless for the day of Christ.
PHILIPPIANS 1:9-10

Lord, as much as I want to, I simply cannot filter all that my child will be exposed to now and in the future. I accept my responsibility to nurture my child, Lord, yet I acknowledge that ultimately, I cannot protect them apart from you.

So I seek your protection over them. I pray you will give my child the spiritual gifts of wisdom and discernment in addition to the other gifts you have designated for them. Increase my child's love for you daily. Help them to be aware of your presence and in love with your Word of truth. And when my child learns what is right, give them courage to stand up for it, wisdom to know how to do that, and faith to know that you are constantly with them.

A FIRM FOUNDATION

*Do not conform to the pattern of this world,
but be transformed by the renewing of your mind.
Then you will be able to test and approve what
God's will is—his good, pleasing and perfect will.*
Romans 12:2

Heavenly Father, help my child to know in the core of their being who they are and whose they are. I ask you to help them take a stand for you even when it means standing against the masses. May they always represent your truth, your teaching, and your directives.

My child cannot possibly know what truth is unless they are grounded in you and have your Word as their foundation. Open their eyes to your truth. Empower my child to discern what is genuinely from you and what is a hollow counterfeit. Daily, fill my child with the renewing of your Spirit so they will not attempt to find this knowledge alone. Grant my child the courage to walk in the truth you impart to them.

PASSION
FOR GOD

MAY MY CHILD HAVE A DEEP DESIRE

TO WORSHIP YOU.

INTIMACY WITH THE LORD

Because your love is better than life,
my lips will glorify you.
PSALM 63:3

Lord God, my heart's desire is for my child to know you intimately and to walk with you consistently. I believe you have created this child for that purpose above all others. You want a relationship with my child.

Please help my child to see, experience, and understand the value of walking through life with you. No other love can compare with the love you give. No one else can meet needs like you do. None can be completely trusted like you can. Please allow my child to see you and know you in this way, and then, Lord, empower them to praise and thank you for everything you have done in their life.

SEEK YOU WHOLEHEARTEDLY

You will seek me and find me
when you seek me with all your heart.
JEREMIAH 29:13

love the image of my child looking for you, Lord. Not
because you are hidden or distant—just the oppo-
site! You promise those who seek you with their whole
heart that they will find you. What a beautiful promise!
Father, I claim that promise for my child.

Lord, my child will be tempted to chase after so
many things—some of them good, and some bad. Yet
none compare with you. I believe you designed each
of us with a hole in our spirit that you alone can fill. O
Father, please help my child to sense this. Lead them
away from that which is false, and instead, grant my
child a heart for you that you will make whole.

PRAISE DESPITE CIRCUMSTANCES

I will extol the LORD at all times;
his praise will always be on my lips.
PSALM 34:1

When my child speaks of you, God, help them to use words that honor and praise you. When they open their mouth to praise your name, may it not be mere lip service, but rather sincere reverence flowing from a heart that adores you and desires to commend you not just for what you have done but also for your very character.

My child will easily praise you when things are going well, Lord. Yet that is not enough! You do not change with our circumstances. For this reason, please lead my child to praise you in the good and the bad. May my child's lips always be filled with praise for the one true God.

THE GREATEST PRIZE

Whom have I in heaven but you?
And earth has nothing I desire besides you.
PSALM 73:25

Life is sometimes difficult to understand, Lord. Yet when all else falls away, you remain…and you are truly all we need. We sometimes get entangled in the chase after material possessions, money, and status, yet those things are not permanent. They provide a false sense of comfort.

This is not so with you. Those who know you and walk with you have all they need. You are the greatest prize, the most valuable possession. Help my child to know this and to understand the value and worth of living a life of intimacy with you. I pray you will be the most important part of my child's life. Be a constant presence and the desire of their heart.

SPIRIT OF GRATITUDE

I will give thanks to you, LORD, with all my heart;
I will tell of all your wonderful deeds. I will
be glad and rejoice in you; I will sing the
praises of your name, O Most High.
PSALM 9:1-2

Lord, my child might be tempted to take credit for their accomplishments and blessings. They might grow to believe that their possessions and gifts are somehow of their own creation. Lord, please keep my child from false pride and self-centered thought.

Instead, Lord, grant my child a deep understanding that all they are, all they will be…these are gifts from your hand. You are the giver. My child is just a recipient. O Lord, give my child a deeply rooted spirit of gratitude. May words of praise and honor for you flow from their lips throughout their lifetime. You have gifted my child with the ability to praise you, and I ask that they always do so. May they boldly bring you honor and glorify your name.

A PASSION FOR PRAISING YOU

*My lips will shout for joy when I sing praise
to you—I whom you have delivered.*
PSALM 71:23

In those moments when life happens and you miraculously extend your hand toward my child, I pray that they would not only recognize what you have done but also stop and give thanks for the way you have delivered them. You will no doubt have many opportunities to intervene on behalf of my child, Lord. Sometimes we see your protective hand, and other times we simply do not. Yet you are still the deliverer.

I thank you on behalf of my child for your continuous provision and protection. My hope is that my child will see and learn of this part of your character and will not be content to just accept it. Instead, help my child to develop a passion for praising you—not just a habit, but a heartfelt worship of their Savior.

COURAGE

MAY MY CHILD BE EMPOWERED
BY FAITH TO BOLDLY FACE
EVERY CHALLENGE.

STRENGTH AND ABILITY THROUGH CHRIST

---

*In all these things we are more than conquerors
through him who loved us.*
ROMANS 8:37

From the moment discouragement sets in, or when the opposition seems too big, Lord, help my child trust that you have equipped them with all they need to face the challenges head-on.

Fear does not need to take root. Your truth does. Bring about constant reminders of your strength and ability. Remind my child as often as is needed that you are equipping them to be victorious. The battles are not their own to conquer. You have already overcome!

GOD'S STRENGTH TO DO ALL THINGS

I can do all this through him who gives me strength.
PHILIPPIANS 4:13

Lord, help my child not to battle against you. Help them to know that you are the God whose strength is unlimited. Your power and understanding exceed anything we can comprehend. Unveil my child's eyes so they can clearly see that you are in control. You fight their battles. They will not fight with their might alone.

Holy Lord, grant my child the humility to follow your leading and the wisdom to give you the honor due your name for the battle's outcome. Raise up within my child the character, wisdom, discernment, actions, and trust necessary to obediently follow your leadership and your plan.

CONFIDENCE TO APPROACH YOU

Let us then approach God's throne of grace
with confidence, so that we may receive mercy
and find grace to help us in our time of need.
HEBREWS 4:16

In moments of need or discouragement, Lord, help my child to remember that you always welcome them— invite them!—into your presence. You will not turn them away. No, you will gladly receive them.

Help my child to learn to depend on you. Help them trust you to meet their needs, and may they never be reluctant to ask you to do so. You long for your children to come to you, seeking whatever they need. You love to provide for your children. Help my child to know that no need is too large or too small to share with you.

RELYING SOLELY ON YOU

---

*Trust in the LORD with all your heart
and lean not on your own understanding.*
PROVERBS 3:5

There will be times, Lord, when my child will face circumstances that feel like roadblocks and dead ends. They will want to know what to do or where to go next, yet that knowledge will seem completely out of reach.

In those times, Lord, please encourage my child not to pull away from you emotionally. Instead, Lord, invite my child to lean into you, draw near to you, and trust you in a deeper and more intimate way. May they rely not on what is seen or understood through human perspective. Instead, help them to depend solely on your heavenly perspective.

ERASE THE FEAR

The LORD is my light and my salvation—
whom shall I fear? The LORD is the stronghold
of my life—of whom shall I be afraid?
PSALM 27:1

Lord, I think of so many leaders in your Word—men and women whom you chose to use in your service to accomplish your purpose. Time and again the obstacles against them appeared to be insurmountable. Certainly, fear was part of their experience in leading your people and fighting for truth.

I believe that you want your people to step into leadership positions for you. Some, you plan to use in big ways, some in smaller, yet all are leading and making a difference in their sphere of influence. However you plan to use my child, pour into them the courage they need to be set apart. Remove any doubt or fear from their mind. My child is yours. Use them as you see fit.

STRONG AND COURAGEOUS

---

*Have I not commanded you? Be strong
and courageous. Do not be afraid; do not
be discouraged, for the LORD your God
will be with you wherever you go.*

JOSHUA 1:9

When fears rise up within my child, Lord, remind them there is no reason to dwell in that state of mind. You will not abandon my child. You will not be taken by surprise. You have seen each moment, and you have already created a plan to intercede on their behalf.

Therefore, Father, help my child to stand firm in the knowledge that the Lord their God will fight for them. You will not allow evil or darkness to overtake them. You will not—you *cannot*—be thwarted. Fill my child with courage, knowing that they are not on their own.

SUPERNATURAL
PEACE

MAY MY CHILD EXPERIENCE YOUR
COMFORT AND CALM ASSURANCE
IN THE MIDST OF LIFE'S STORMS.

YOU ARE TRUSTWORTHY

You will keep in perfect peace those whose
minds are steadfast, because they trust in you.
Trust in the LORD forever, for the LORD,
the LORD himself, is the Rock eternal.
ISAIAH 26:3-4

May your perfect peace fill the space in my child's mind that would otherwise be clouded by fear and anxiety. In the presence of your light, the darkness must flee. I am asking on my child's behalf that you remove any thoughts that would prevent them from sensing, knowing, and experiencing your light.

Trust is formed through repeated action. Time and again, O Lord, you have shown yourself to be true to your word. May your promises for peace beyond what we can comprehend, for peace in spite of circumstances, permeate every crevice of my child's mind.

ONLY PEACE REMAINS

Peace I leave with you; my peace I give you.
I do not give to you as the world gives. Do not let
your hearts be troubled and do not be afraid.
JOHN 14:27

Lord, you alone are able to see inside my child's heart and mind. You alone know what could bring fear in each chapter of their life. In every circumstance, Lord, help my child to take those thoughts captive to you and bring them under your authority. Save my child from drowning in a sea of fear. Instead, may they dwell in your presence, where there is nothing to fear and where there is an abundance of peace. Help my child to leave everything in your hand.

GOD HAS OVERCOME

———————

*I have told you these things, so that in me
you may have peace. In this world you will have
trouble. But take heart! I have overcome the world.*

JOHN 16:33

When we know an outcome, peace abounds. O Lord, you have shared the final outcome! Therefore, every time pressure or distress threaten to overwhelm my child, may those things never be allowed to take up residence. Instead, Lord, may the knowledge of your victory and your promise to overcome the world—your plan for mankind—remove all fear.

There are no unknown outcomes with you. Not a one. If my child begins to doubt this, I pray the truth of your Word would ring true in their mind. You have overcome. Trouble may come, but it will not be permanent. You will be victorious!

REMOVE EACH FEAR

*May the Lord of peace himself give you
peace at all times and in every way.*
2 Thessalonians 3:16

We fear so many different things, Lord. From complex fears that are tied to our baggage, to fears that seem completely unlinked to any past experiences… who can make sense of it? Lord, you are not the author of fear. You do not desire your people to live in fear or to suffer its crippling effects. The more we fear, the less we trust you to meet all our needs and protect us.

Lord, remove my child's fears, and grant them your peace that passes all understanding. Storms may rage around us, yet I ask you to provide a shelter for my child in the storms. Allow my child to dwell in your peace in the midst of chaos…even when it doesn't seem to make sense.

GOD'S BLESSING

The LORD bless you and keep you; the LORD
make his face shine on you and be gracious to you;
the LORD turn his face toward
you and give you peace.
NUMBERS 6:24-26

What parent doesn't desire to see the Lord pour out his blessings on their children? Singing these words of blessing over my child brings chills.

Bless my child, Lord, and keep them safe in your strong hands. Shine your light of love on them, and extend to them your goodness and grace. Turn my child's gaze toward you, and hold it there so they will not be distracted or pulled away from you. Grant my child a life of intimacy with you, which brings peace regardless of their circumstances. O Lord, may my child know such blessing now and always!

LET CHRIST RULE

Let the peace of Christ rule in your hearts,
since as members of one body you were
called to peace. And be thankful.
COLOSSIANS 3:15

No one is better equipped to rule in my child's heart than you are! Lord, reign in their heart. The decision to submit to you is theirs to make because you have given them this gift of free choice. O God, may my child choose to follow you every day as their Lord and Savior.

Help my child remember that when you rule, you lead. There are so many reasons why we should submit to your direction, Lord. You see all things, know all things, and can do all things. Why would we believe for even a moment that we were better suited to lead than you are? Lead my child well. I am so thankful for your hand upon them.

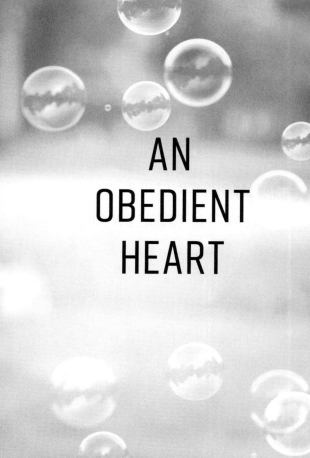

AN
OBEDIENT
HEART

MAY MY CHILD'S HIGHEST PRIORITY

ALWAYS BE TO FOLLOW YOU.

DEEPLY ROOTED FAITH

---

*I have hidden your word in my heart
that I might not sin against you.*
PSALM 119:11

Lord, please hide your Word deep within my child's heart. I want to lead them in the right direction, and yet ultimately, I know that unless your Word takes root, no effort on my part holds any value. This is all about you.

I am asking that you would keep your Word at the forefront of my child's mind. I pray that you would use it to guide them and guard them from anything that would lead them into temptation or sin. May your Word illumine the path you have laid out for them. Father, may they receive your Word not as a list of restrictions, but as you intend it to be—a love letter. Lord, may they fall more in love with you and your Word every day of their life.

YOUR WILL ABOVE SELF

I desire to do your will, my God;
your law is within my heart.
PSALM 40:8

Those who desire to do your will demonstrate that they cherish you, Lord God. They have stored up your laws like a treasure. They seek to live for you.

I will do my part to share your law with my child, but Lord, beyond that, I ask you to help my child to love you so deeply that this becomes their own passionate desire—not just to please their earthly parent, but to please their Father in heaven. May they pursue you and conform to your will and purpose in their day-to-day life.

A LIFE OF SERVICE

Fear the LORD and serve him faithfully
with all your heart; consider what
great things he has done for you.
1 SAMUEL 12:24

My greatest desire for my child is for them to know you, love you, and serve you. Our love for you grows as we see who you are and become aware of your presence in our lives. May my child see and understand. Impress upon their heart and mind the countless times you have interceded on their behalf and have provided for them and blessed them. Open their eyes to see these things. Use their memory to hold them.

You do not change like the tides. You are constant. Please empower my child to live an unchanging, faithful, thankful, and devoted life for you, the one true God.

A LIFE OF TRANSPARENCY

Create in me a pure heart, O God,
and renew a steadfast spirit within me.
PSALM 51:10

Lord, your Word is clear that we are all sinners. I recognize that this includes my child. Heavenly Father, I also know that you are a holy God. You will not dwell where sin abides.

Please give my child a desire to live a life of transparency with you. May they never try to hide their sin. Instead, may they be willing to confess it to you, knowing that you can wash them and make them clean in your sight. Lord, give my child a heart that seeks after you and not sin. Mold their spirit so that every day it becomes more like yours.

A HEART LIKE YOURS

May these words of my mouth
and this meditation of my heart
be pleasing in your sight, LORD,
my Rock and my Redeemer.
PSALM 19:14

Things hidden in the mind and heart are bound to be displayed through word and action. No wonder they are so important to you, Lord!

Despite our tendency toward selfishness and sin, please give my child a mind that values what you value, a heart that breaks for what breaks yours, and a will that desires your will above all others. Take my child's thoughts captive to your Word. Give them a heart that is tender and good. May their thought life and their actions glorify and please you, God.

GOD'S TEMPLE

Do you not know that your bodies are temples of the
Holy Spirit, who is in you, whom you have received
from God? You are not your own; you were bought
at a price. Therefore honor God with your bodies.
1 CORINTHIANS 6:19-20

My child does not belong to me. My child's body does not belong to them. My child's body belongs to the King of kings. You created it, Lord, to be a temple or dwelling place for your Spirit. You paid the ultimate price for my child. You gave your life so that my child could be freed from the bondage of sin. The price was so high, and yet out of love, you paid it.

Therefore I ask you to lead my child in ways that reflect that gift. May my child's life and body honor you, Lord. May they live in a way that glorifies you. Help others to see and experience you through my child's words and actions.

RELATIONSHIPS

MAY MY CHILD HAVE GODLY
CONNECTIONS WITH
FRIENDS, MENTORS, AND
THEIR FUTURE SPOUSE.

GOD-HONORING RELATIONSHIPS

Be devoted to one another in love.
Honor one another above yourselves.
ROMANS 12:10

I have seen how easy it is to be consumed by self and how devastating that can be in relationships of every kind. Lord, please free my child from the tyranny of self. Help them to find healthy, God-centered men and women to walk with through this life. Place strategically in their life those who can encourage them in their walk with you and redirect them to you when they are tempted to stray.

Lead my child into loving relationships that honor you and others. May they not focus on living for self, but on loving others well and showing others their value and worth. In honoring others, Lord, my child will be honoring you.

HEALTHY COMPANIONS

---

*The LORD God said, "It is not good for the man to
be alone. I will make a helper suitable for him."*
GENESIS 2:18

Lord, you did not intend for mankind to walk through
life alone. We need and crave the companionship
of others. I know that at some point, this desire for
human companionship and partnership will surface in
my child's life. I ask you to prepare the right partner for
my child, the right companion. You know best. As my
child and their future partner grow, help them to make
you the center of their individual lives and the focus of
their relationship.

In the meantime, Lord, please keep my child and
their future partner under your protective hand. Protect
them from making choices that will bring hurt, challenges,
and baggage into their relationship. Pour into
them a commitment to each other and the covenant
they will enter with you.

GODLY FRIENDS AND MENTORS

---

*If either of them falls down, one can help
the other up. But pity anyone who falls
and has no one to help them up.*
ECCLESIASTES 4:10

Heavenly Father, I ask that at every point in my child's life, you would bring to them people who love and adore you. People who follow you as Lord of their lives and bask in the understanding that you are their Savior. Help these men and women establish godly friendships with my child.

I also know how valuable mentors are and how much my child will need them. I cannot fill this position. So Lord, would you please handpick these mentors to come alongside my child and encourage them to walk with you and live in accordance with your will?

CHOOSING TO PARTNER
WITH A BELIEVER

Do not be yoked together with unbelievers.
For what do righteousness and wickedness
have in common? Or what fellowship
can light have with darkness?
2 CORINTHIANS 6:14

You designed us to crave relationships with you and with one another. Lord, my child will benefit from choosing a mate who is like-minded and committed to you. In such a partnership, much can be accomplished, and the entire household can be devoted to you.

Please help my child not to give their heart to one who does not know you or walk with you. Even now, I ask you to begin preparing their heart and the heart of their future spouse for each other. I ask you to guard and guide their path through life and toward each other.

A FUTURE SPOUSE

Though one may be overpowered, two can defend
themselves. A cord of three strands
is not quickly broken.
ECCLESIASTES 4:12

Relationships are so important, Lord. I pray specifically for my child's future mate. I ask you to bring this person into my child's life at the right time. Help my child know that this person is a good fit for them and not try to force a fit. Lord, I pray this mate will love you above all others and have a deep, healthy love for my child. I ask that the same would be true for my child: that they would love you above all others and place their mate second.

Heavenly Father, you bless us when we live in obedience to you. May my child and their mate always remember that you are part of their marriage and include you in every decision. Bind their hearts to your heart.

LOVE DISPLAYED IN ALL RELATIONSHIPS

May the Lord make your love increase and overflow
for each other and for everyone else.
1 THESSALONIANS 3:12

Lord, please empower my child to love others actively and lavishly, and teach my child to receive love from others too. In their school, in their home, in their job, and in each relationship they develop, I ask that the love you shower upon them would overflow as they demonstrate love for others.

No doubt, Father, this kind of love doesn't always mesh with the way the world would love. Let your demonstration of love—not the world's version of it—be the model my child follows. Let your heart lead the way.

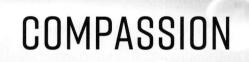

COMPASSION

MAY MY CHILD SEE VALUE IN OTHERS
AND INVEST IN PEOPLE WITH
A HEART OF EMPATHY.

SELFLESS LIVING

In everything, do to others what you would have them do to you, for this sums up the Law and the Prophets.
MATTHEW 7:12

This world promotes living for self, not living for you and loving others well. O Lord, please protect my child from being caught up in that lie. Lord, my child surely knows how they want to be treated. I pray you would give them a heart that beats like yours. May their heart be filled with compassion, just as yours is.

Lord, may my child think less of themselves and more of others. Show them how to be game changers in other people's lives. Keep them looking at the many blessings and unbounded grace they have received so they may share your blessings and grace with others. Open their heart and mind to your leading.

SEEING THE NEEDS OF OTHERS

---

*This is what the L*ORD* Almighty said:*
"Administer true justice; show mercy and
compassion to one another. Do not oppress the
widow or the fatherless, the foreigner or the
poor. Do not plot evil against each other."
ZECHARIAH 7:9-10

Lord, lead my child to see the needs of those in our community, nation, and world. Help my child to know what godly justice, mercy, and compassion look like. I love my child, yet I know that at their very core lies a selfish nature, one that does not reflect your goodness and does not lead to anything righteous and good.

Yet you are a God who does not leave us at our worst, but instead transforms us into your likeness. Form within my child a desire to help those in need and to champion those who are weak. Plant your seeds of love and care in my child's heart. Nurture them. Continually fill them with all they need to pour out your love.

A HEART OF EMPATHY

Rejoice with those who rejoice;
mourn with those who mourn.
ROMANS 12:15

God, help my child to celebrate and rejoice in other people's victories, accomplishments, and blessings. Remove any thoughts of jealousy, resentment, or entitlement that might try to rise up in my child. Instead, help my child to truly celebrate and honor those relationships by rejoicing with their friends' and family's blessings and accomplishments.

Help my child never to become flippant or dismissive of those who are in pain or suffering loss. Place within them a heart of godly empathy and compassion that grieves with those who are grieving. A heart that can be completely present and provide comfort to those who are hurting.

CLOTHED IN COMPASSION

As God's chosen people, holy and dearly loved,
clothe yourselves with compassion, kindness,
humility, gentleness and patience.
Colossians 3:12

The fruit of your Spirit seems to be so rare today and yet is so desperately needed, Lord. I know you desire this kind of fruit from my child. It starts with knowing that you love them dearly, you have chosen them, and you declare them holy. O Lord, may this awareness permeate every fiber of their being. May they walk near you, seek you, and hold your character in such high regard that they begin to live more and more like you!

Give my child a heart of compassion for everyone they encounter. And may they always relate to others with kindness. Remove from my child any attitude of pride or superiority; instead, fill them with a humble spirit. May they abound in love and treat others gently and patiently.

COMFORT IN CHAOS

Praise be to the God and Father of our Lord Jesus Christ, the Father of compassion and the God of all comfort, who comforts us in all our troubles, so that we can comfort those in any trouble with the comfort we ourselves receive from God.

2 CORINTHIANS 1:3-4

Father, I often wish that my child could be free of pain, that they could know joy without suffering the hurts of this life. But I realize that our sorrows provide opportunities for us to know you more deeply than we ever would if our lives were always easy.

So this is my request: Instead of preventing the pain, please help my child to be aware of your presence in the midst of pain. Comfort my child. Bring peace and hope into the chaos and hurts that will inevitably arise. Then in turn, Lord, help my child use their hurts and hard times to bring life and hope to the lives of others who are suffering too.

LIGHT AND HOPE

All of you, be like-minded, be sympathetic,
love one another, be compassionate and humble.
1 Peter 3:8

My child will undoubtedly encounter those who think and act differently than they do, many of whom will have no desire to walk with you. In every situation, help my child to look for the good in people, to find something admirable to encourage in the life of everyone they meet.

Give my child eyes of compassion and gentleness that they may be a beacon of the hope and light that only your truth provides. Save my child from attitudes of superiority and entitlement, and empower them instead to live out the characteristics of Jesus as a true Christ-follower. By living this way, may my child be a magnet who draws others to you.

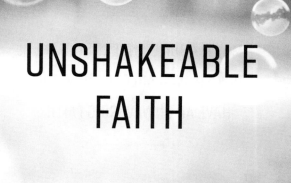

UNSHAKEABLE
FAITH

MAY MY CHILD UNDERSTAND THE
POWER AVAILABLE TO THEM AND
HAVE AN UNWAVERING FAITH.

MOUNTAIN MOVER

---

*Truly I tell you, if you have faith as small as
a mustard seed, you can say to this mountain,
"Move from here to there," and it will move.
Nothing will be impossible for you.*
MATTHEW 17:20

You, O Lord, not only form the mountains—you can move them! Heavenly Father, I know that goodness and blessings are not the only things my child will experience. Life is always a mixture of good and bad. Yet you are always good. You are capable of things we cannot even begin to fathom.

Throughout my child's life, please continue to reveal yourself as the mountain mover. Whenever my child comes to a hurdle or faces an obstacle, please display your powerful hand. Lord, I ask that my child will always come to you, remembering that you can use everything for good. Everything. Every hurt. Every need. Every circumstance. Anything will move when you command it to. Lord, may they see your hand at work in each chapter of their life, in Jesus's name.

GOD OF THE IMPOSSIBLE

"'If you can'?" said Jesus.
"Everything is possible for one who believes."
MARK 9:23

Each time my child feels overwhelmed by this life and by the barriers that come up against them—messages of defeat, messages that would squelch and demolish the hope that is available through you, Lord—please silence those messages. Prevent the weight of discouragement from taking up residence in my child.

Instead of discouragement, Lord, remind my child that you are the God of possibilities! You are the one with whom nothing is impossible! There is always reason for hope because of your miraculous hand. So strengthen their faith and hope in you, Lord. All they need is to believe in you.

EMPOWERED FOR A PURPOSE

*Now to him who is able to do immeasurably more
than all we ask or imagine, according to his power
that is at work within us, to him be glory.*
EPHESIANS 3:20-21

Your ways are so much higher than our ways, Lord. Your understanding of situations is so different from our limited perspectives. You create everything according to your plan and purpose.

Lord, my child may think they are unable to achieve the things you have prepared for them to accomplish. Help them to know that you will empower them to achieve every part of your plan. Assure them that they will not be acting alone; you will dwell in them and work through them. Lord, fill them with your Spirit and use them for your glory.

STRONG FAITH

---

*In addition to all this, take up the shield
of faith, with which you can extinguish
all the flaming arrows of the evil one.*
EPHESIANS 6:16

How can my child remain in this world and not become swayed by the things in it that oppose you? How can my child walk through each day with confidence when they are constantly bombarded with information that contradicts your Word and our hope in you?

Lord, strengthen their faith. You know what is needed to make it grow. Father, help it flourish. May they stand firm in the power of your Word. May they read it, absorb it, meditate on it, and use it. Raise up within them a faith in you so strong that it will protect them from all the attacks of the evil one. Please cultivate that kind of faith—a mountain-moving faith—within my child.

BELIEF AS THEIR ANCHOR

If you believe, you will receive
whatever you ask for in prayer.
MATTHEW 21:22

Lord, the hopelessness in our world spills over into our hearts if we are not completely grounded in you. When hopelessness threatens to take control of my child's thoughts and decisions, may the truth of your Word be an anchor for them: "If you believe…"

Wherever doubt would creep in, Lord, remove it. In its place, fill my child with assurance that you are listening to each prayer, that you are aware of each need. Father, may my child know you as the God of miracles. Help them to know they can always bring their requests to you, O loving heavenly Father.

AN UNSHAKEABLE FOUNDATION

I have trusted in the LORD and have not faltered.
PSALM 26:1

In good times and bad times, Lord, hold my child fast in your strong hands. Grant to them a strong faith, a solid foundation on which they can build their life. Set that foundation on your unshakeable truth, which does not shift like the sand, even during life's fiercest storms. Regardless of circumstances, may my child be secure in your presence. Reveling in your love.

Be the steadfast certainty that they need. Unchanging. Dependable. Be my child's immoveable lifeline. Plant their feet firmly on the rock of salvation, that they may never slip away from it.

SAFETY

MAY MY CHILD BE COVERED BY
YOUR PHYSICAL, SPIRITUAL, AND
EMOTIONAL PROTECTION, LORD.

PROTECTION AGAINST EVIL

The Lord is faithful, and he will strengthen you
and protect you from the evil one.
2 THESSALONIANS 3:3

O Lord, would you please do what only you can do and place my child under your protective hand? My heart is tempted to worry about my child. And in my worry, I attempt to control what I have no ability to control! But this child is yours—a gift you have loaned to me, Father.

No doubt the evil one will do anything to steal your children away from you and cause trouble and hurt. Yet you are stronger, Lord. Who can pluck anything from your hand? Not even the powers of hell stand a chance against you! So I place my precious child in your hands. Protect them and provide strength through every battle, in Jesus's name.

PLACED IN YOUR HANDS

God is our refuge and strength,
an ever-present help in trouble.
PSALM 46:1

God, you are the ever-present help for my child's life. You can handle every need in every part of my child's being. You care about each piece of the puzzle, and your care is even greater—by far!—than what I know to be true of you.

Lord, I place my child's physical, emotional, and spiritual needs in your hands. There is no better place for my child to be. Your love is so great, and your knowledge and wisdom are so vast. You know just what to do. You know each intricate detail. Thank you, Lord, for caring about my child this way. Thank you for your promises of protection and provision.

EMOTIONAL PROTECTION

You are my hiding place; you will protect me from
trouble and surround me with songs of deliverance.
PSALM 32:7

I lift up to you my child's emotional needs. I know my child so well, and yet there are still so many aspects that I miss—that I don't understand or see. You see it all, don't you, Lord? You know every detail of this child you created.

When my child faces rejection, remind them that you embrace them wholeheartedly. They are chosen and dearly loved. When my child experiences relationships that don't live up to their expectations or promises, remind them that they have a relationship with a heavenly Father who is faithful and keeps his word. When my child is told that they are not enough or lack ability or skills, remind them that they are designed perfectly—a masterpiece! Protect, surround, and deliver my child, Lord.

HEALTH AND REST

In peace I will lie down and sleep,
for you alone, Lord, make me dwell in safety.
PSALM 4:8

Sleep comes only when we feel safe enough to rest.
Lord, I ask you to bless my child now and always
with the rest they need to maintain their health. Father,
you alone bring that type of peace and assurance to the
hearts of parents and children who belong to you.

As you bring sleep to my child, I pray you will protect their mind from anything that would bring fear or
evil into their room. I pray you will grant my child the
sweetness of rest that comes only from your presence.
And then, Lord, as my child awakes, may they rise in
the morning feeling refreshed and ready for a new day
ordained by you.

PROTECTION OF THEIR MIND

He will cover you with his feathers,
and under his wings you will find refuge;
his faithfulness will be your shield and rampart.
PSALM 91:4

I will continually bring my child before you, Lord, asking for your handprints to be all over their life. Lord, I specifically ask that you would be with my child's mind. The mind is so fragile, isn't it? Will you protect my child's mind? Imprint your Word and your truth on it. Help the Word to develop deep roots of faith.

Please protect my child's thoughts when they experience difficult circumstances. Don't allow the devil or any evil thought to steal their focus from you. Instead, Lord, bring your Word to the forefront of their mind as the shield and defense you intended it to be. May your presence ever be my child's refuge and strength.

PHYSICAL PROTECTION

---

*I lift up my eyes to the mountains—where does
my help come from? My help comes from the LORD,
the Maker of heaven and earth. He will not let your
foot slip—he who watches over you will not slumber.*
PSALM 121:1-3

There is no place my child can go—from the highest
heights to the deepest depths—where you have not
already been and where you will not be. You are present with them. When staying on your path is partic-
ularly challenging for my child, I ask you to remind
them that you will not permit their foot to slip. You
will not stop providing help. You never take a break
from watching over your children. No, you stay awake,
like the shepherd watching over their flock. Protecting.
Leading. Guiding.

Thank you for placing your protection over my
child.

JOY

MAY MY CHILD KNOW
THE JOY AND HOPE OF THE LORD.

A REFUGE OF JOY

Let all who take refuge in you be glad; let them
ever sing for joy. Spread your protection over them,
that those who love your name may rejoice in you.
PSALM 5:11

Jesus, I love to hear my child's laughter. Many little things can bring it on. My heart expands when their happiness bubbles up as our family plays games, jokes, and sings songs. I'm grateful when my child expresses their unique personality in the safety of our love. Today I pray for my child to know the gladness of being your child, to experience the mercy of your name, and to trust the familiarity of your presence.

Cover my child, Lord. Spread your protection over them so that in the safety of your love, they never hold back their delight…for their sake, for mine, and so your heart, too, can expand at the sound of your child's joy.

JOY-FILLED

The Lord has done great things for us,
and we are filled with joy.
PSALM 126:3

Lord, as blessings arise, I love to point out each one to my child. Give them the desire to honor all you've given and to anticipate with joy all you will do throughout their lifetime. May their heart be filled with appreciation for your care so that even in hard times they will see new possibilities in you.

As you bless my child, their spirit of gladness overflows into their words and actions. I've witnessed this in the compassion and wonder they express. I've been encouraged by their eagerness to share without expecting things in return. Already they are living out a joyful faith. I realize with awe that this is another great thing you have done. Thank you, Lord.

DELIGHT

---

*Trust in the LORD and do good; dwell in the land
and enjoy safe pasture. Take delight in the LORD,
and he will give you the desires of your heart.*
PSALM 37:3-4

God, thank you for calling my child and me to you
and embracing us with a loving Father's acceptance.
Help us to trust in you as our foundation, our center,
and our compass for doing good. I want my child to be
able to make their way through life's valleys and peaks
with a sense of safety and assurance. From this certainty
comes a delight and freedom like no other.

Thank you for allowing my child to trust, express,
and run toward the desires of their heart in your
strength and with your blessing. When others challenge that desire or try to turn it toward a worldly purpose, intercede for my child so they can reclaim their
unaffected joy in you. Give me wisdom to see and
encourage their desires as well, Lord, so will I celebrate
your vision for my child.

JUST BECAUSE

Let them praise his name with dancing
and make music to him with timbrel and harp.
PSALM 149:3

What could give me more joy than seeing my child express their joy with full abandon just because? It's something to behold! They aren't performing. They aren't seeking approval. They aren't laughing, singing, and dancing because they were told to. They are simply happy in the purest sense and allowing their actions to mirror that joy. This is from your heart of delight, Lord. You instill in us both reverence and revelry. What a gift! In fact, as you show me through my child what unhindered delight and playful praise look like, you are reminding me how I used to be able to do that without self-judgment. You are allowing my child to lead me back to praising you just because.

God, may my child always offer you the music of their laughter and worship, and may I join in with a glad, glad heart.

RESTORED JOY

Restore to me the joy of your salvation
and grant me a willing spirit, to sustain me.
PSALM 51:12

Lord, thank you for giving your children the security to experience vulnerability and joy. I'm relearning how to do that with a childlike faith. Becoming a parent has given me a front-row seat to watch the glow and beauty and even strength of innocence as you intended.

When my first response is to quiet my child or squelch their first response of joy, Lord, please release me from my concerns. Free me from the have-tos and filters I've adopted that limit my heart's response to your gift of salvation. I pray you will preserve my child's abiding belief and gladness. Restore to me a limitless capacity for joy in my faith so that when my child erupts with delight, I am the first one to join in and celebrate the gift—and you, the Giver of life.

IF YOU'RE HAPPY
AND YOU KNOW IT

Is anyone happy? Let them sing songs of praise.
JAMES 5:13

I used to think the song "If You're Happy and You Know It" was too simple. Yet now as a parent, I love encouraging my child to respond to happiness with raucous gratitude. I want them to clap their hands, stomp their feet, shout hallelujah, and praise your name for the miracle of being truly beloved. Bring it on!

Jesus, let joy rain down on my family. Life is hard, and yet doing life together and in communion with you is a gift. Help my child to understand this now so they will feel the hope more than the hardship. When they experience a setback, give them a spark that ignites their joy. Turn their downcast eyes and downhearted spirit upward. And turn their frown upside down. (I just had to say it, Lord.)

PRAYER

MAY MY CHILD KNOW HOW TO

COMMUNICATE WITH THEIR ABBA.

ALWAYS OPEN

The LORD has heard my cry for mercy;
the LORD accepts my prayer.
PSALM 6:9

Lord, my child longs for acceptance from their peers and even from strangers now that much of the world is accessible online. They want their words to be heard, and they struggle when their opinions and emotions get lost or are dismissed in the din. God, help my child to know that their words are priceless, that their thoughts matter, and that you always hear and accept their cries. Instill in them the confidence to come to you with all things and never to think that anything is too small or too serious. I want them to know and believe that your heart is always open. May they experience this truth and connection regularly in their young and maturing life.

HUMBLE PRAYERS

When you pray, go into your room, close the
door and pray to your Father, who is unseen.
Then your Father, who sees what is
done in secret, will reward you.
MATTHEW 6:6

The special connection between you and your children is a joy I love to share with my child. I want them to experience intimate, free, safe, and personal time with you. So much of what they witness in the world is about performance and being noticed.

Jesus, call to them in the joyful potential of each morning and the calm of evening. Beckon their heart to be open and humble so they bring their needs and love to you in private. I want them to believe unequivocally that you will hold as treasures the prayers they whisper, think, ponder in their heart, or cry through tears. Humility does not cast us further from your presence or priorities; it ushers us into the immediacy of your unconditional embrace. Thank you, Jesus.

RAISED IN LOVE

The prayer offered in faith will make the sick person well; the Lord will raise them up... The prayer of a righteous person is powerful and effective.

JAMES 5:15-16

As my child grows and takes steps toward becoming who they are, I cannot wait for them to discover the power of their prayers as a believer. God, please bless my child with a healthy understanding of the strength behind their petitions as they also learn the art of lifting praises for your mercies. It's never too soon for them to learn the responsibility and might of being a person of prayer.

In times of pain, illness, or upset, Lord, lift them up in health and righteousness. When they fall, I pray you will bring them to their feet so next time they will first rush to bow at yours. Worrying and waiting or being stubborn or stoic will not serve them well...but being prayerful will make them powerful as a child of God.

A WAY TO PRAY

Our Father in heaven, hallowed be your name,
your kingdom come, your will be done,
on earth as it is in heaven.
MATTHEW 6:9-10

Thank you for the beloved prayer you gave us. It provides a simple way to approach you as our Father in heaven. Instill in my child a reverence for you as I teach them this in word and action. I long to give them a path to prayer and relationship with you. As I teach my child to know and love your name and to hold it as sacred, I pray you will give them a heart-sense of your guidance and your hope for them and the world.

Bless my child with an ability to recognize your will when they hear it, read it, and receive it in response to their earnest prayers. Bless me with this ability too, dear Lord, so I may parent in your will and enter prayer with love for your hallowed name.

DAILY BREAD OF LIFE

---

*Give us today our daily bread. And forgive us
our debts, as we also have forgiven our debtors.*
MATTHEW 6:11-12

Lord, spark a lifelong and life-giving conversation with
my child's heart. I'm grateful for the tie of tenderness you have with each of your children. Help me to
share with my child what it means to have an ongoing,
real-time discussion with you and how it will encourage, guide, and shape their path. Impress on my child's
heart their dependence on you for basic needs, from
the first bite of breakfast to the deep breaths they take
as they fall asleep.

Cultivate in them a spirit that prays for all things,
including your forgiveness and the power and compassion to forgive others. God, there is no greater lesson I
can share with my child than how to turn to you as our
sustenance and our bread of life for every need, every
hope, every day.

SEEK AND FIND

So I say to you: Ask and it will be given to you;
seek and you will find; knock and the door will be
opened to you. For everyone who asks receives;
the one who seeks finds; and to the one who
knocks, the door will be opened.
LUKE 11:9-10

God, I pray for my child to be a seeker. Give them a desire to find you. Oh, how I hope they always experience you and your presence as their true home. A home they can approach with hope and anticipation as they prepare to knock on the door. With reverence and openness, may they ask each question they have when friends, the world, or even their family members confuse them, or when challenges cause them to doubt.

Instill in them a curious nature that nudges them to ask for faith, answers, provision, and ways to know and praise you. Now they try to solve troubles in their own power. May one day soon their first response be to pray, ask, and seek so they will be blessed to find the light of your presence and truth.

LOVE

MAY MY CHILD KNOW YOUR LOVE

AND SHARE IT WITH OTHERS.

CHOOSING LIFE AND LOVE

Now choose life, so that you and your children may
live and that you may love the LORD your God,
listen to his voice, and hold fast to him.
DEUTERONOMY 30:19-20

God, I envision my child encircled by your love and surrounded by others who encourage and nourish their faith. In the center, they stand with their eyes and arms lifted up to you...a gesture of offering, prayer, devotion, openness to your Word, and dependence.

I don't want my child to believe the things I do simply to please me. I want them to love you passionately because I know this relationship and spiritual journey becomes everything. It is a thread of compassion that weaves around and through all relationships, conversations, choices, and dreams. And it is their unhindered connection to you, merciful Creator.

LOVE ALWAYS

Love does not delight in evil but rejoices
with the truth. It always protects, always trusts,
always hopes, always perseveres.
1 CORINTHIANS 13:6-7

When I sign a letter "love always," I smile. My hope rises and becomes a prayer for me, for the world, and most of all for my child. Lord, give to my child a love that is for you and of you. A love that is eternal in scope and purpose. A love that does not celebrate anything that demeans, defiles, or distracts from you but instead searches for and illuminates truth and goodness. Grow my child into a person whose love for you propels them into actions of mercy and righteousness. May they protect, trust, hope, and persevere because that is what your love within them does every single day. This is my prayer for my child, Lord. After all, what could be more important and influential than a life that mirrors your love always?

FOR THE GOOD

We know that in all things God works
for the good of those who love him, who have
been called according to his purpose.
ROMANS 8:28

Lord, you and I both know this child of mine will sometimes falter. I pray this only makes them more grateful for your grace and more eager to extend mercy to others. They will sometimes question more than they praise. I pray this deepens their trust in you because you won't leave them hanging. They will sometimes challenge my parenting and decisions. May this testing reveal that guidance is love.

And Lord, they will sometimes question why they are on this earth. Even though it could be a season of struggle, I pray that in this, too, you will work for the good you set in motion. You will refine them, speak to their spirit, and fill them with the conviction and joy of one who is called by name for your purpose.

THE LOVE YOU GIVE

My command is this: Love each other as I
have loved you. Greater love has no one than this:
to lay down one's life for one's friends.
JOHN 15:12-13

Show my child and me how to love others, Jesus. When we wander through a store and interact with strangers. When we reach out to neighbors with encouragement. When we gather as a family and take inventory of how everyone is doing. When we stumble and sincerely ask forgiveness from those we've hurt. When we sacrifice in your name a personal want or comfort for the well-being and need of another.

The world will say sacrifice is loss. May my child discover that sacrifice is about love and progress. It's about coming alongside another and experiencing the power of unconditional love to move forward, unite, and uplift others in your will and wonder.

I SEE YOU

---

*No one has ever seen God; but if we love one
another, God lives in us and his love is made
complete in us. This is how we know that we live
in him and he in us: He has given us of his Spirit.*
1 John 4:12-13

There are so many experiences, friendships, and trials ahead for my child. Their life is unfinished business in the big picture, yet in them, Lord, your love is made complete. They are a vessel filled with the Spirit and prepared to overflow with your affection for others even in their youth.

Help them to notice your mercies pouring forth from others so every part of their being cries, "I see you, Lord, I see you." May they know you as the source of a love beyond our human capacity. Your face shines in the joy of a fellow human. Your compassion radiates in the kindness of and toward strangers and neighbors. Give my child a heart so big for others that every day flows with expressions of who you are.

COMFORT THEM, LORD

---

*If you have any encouragement from being united
with Christ, if any comfort from his love, if any
common sharing in the Spirit, if any tenderness
and compassion, then make my joy complete
by being like-minded, having the same love,
being one in spirit and of one mind.*
PHILIPPIANS 2:1-2

My child will hurt, Lord. I won't always be around them or be the one they come to with their wounded pride or broken heart. When they come to me now, remind me to turn their eyes to you, the compassionate Savior. My child's journey will include experiences of discord and separation in the body of Christ and in their relationships with others. Help them remember the comfort they have felt in your care so they can draw from it, speak from it, and respond from it rather than become divisive or hopeless. And when they are alone and afraid or troubled and unsure, soothe them, Jesus, with the sweet assurance and comfort of your precious love. Let it surround them like a familiar, tender embrace.

HOPE FOR
A FUTURE

MAY MY CHILD SEE
THE LIGHT OF HOPE ON
THE PATH AHEAD.

ALWAYS HOPE

---

*There is surely a future hope for you,
and your hope will not be cut off.*
PROVERBS 23:18

I hold my child tight. The love I have for this kid is profound, Lord. It is hard for me to imagine anyone loving them as much as I do or being a mightier advocate than I am for this being. That is, except for you, Lord. My feelings are mere droplets compared to your vast ocean of love, care, and concern for them. You know the path and future prepared for them. You will not abandon them, nor will you sever them from your love.

Thank you for the gift of hope that assures this parent's heart and inspires my beloved child today and tomorrow. I'm grateful that even when they're not leaning into my presence, they are secure in your embrace and strength.

LEGACY OF THE LORD

—————

The plans of the Lord stand firm forever,
the purposes of his heart through all generations.
Psalm 33:11

Lord, your influence, significance, and love don't ebb and flow. They are consistent forces for your will and purpose. Just as treasured heirlooms and stories are passed between generations in our family, so too are the treasured purposes of your heart. Lord, I pray my child will sense those purposes and be guided, inspired, moved, and convicted by them.

Does my child's heart reflect your own? I pray it does. God, I lift them up today with renewed hope for their future. Their future will be the one you created for them, shaped by the legacy, purposes, and plans you establish as a foundation for all generations.

ENOUGH

Do not worry about tomorrow,
for tomorrow will worry about itself.
Each day has enough trouble of its own.
MATTHEW 6:34

Jesus, when my child is anxious, I pray you will soothe their spirit so their breath can match your breath of peace. Calm their concerns about upcoming plans, next-day tasks, or anticipated troubles. When I see their wide stare of uncertainty or fear, my heart breaks. I assure them and hug them. Sometimes I want to resolve the challenge even if it's not a bad thing. Yet their tomorrows will inevitably include obstacles. My first impulse should not be to preempt their difficulty but to pray and lead them to your feet by example. Thank you for turning my child's heart of uncertainty into a vessel filled with the balm of your grace. In this way, each day my child will have enough peace of their own.

UNFOLDING CONVERSATION

Your statutes are wonderful; therefore I obey them.
The unfolding of your words gives light;
it gives understanding to the simple.
PSALM 119:129-130

I t is a joy to see my child discover your still, small voice, God. Through your Word and the witness of faith-filled people, they are drawn to your heart. I hear their simple and earnest prayers when they are scared, happy, unsure, or seeking help for friends. The prayer of my heart is for my child's future to be shaped by the unfolding of your written and Spirit-whispered words and to be illuminated by the truths you speak into their life.

As seasons of youth turn to seasons of adulthood, may my child cling to your statutes. Not out of fear or ritual, but out of an expanding delight in and intimacy with their caring Creator. May they always talk with you and seek the love and wisdom you use to light their path and purpose.

GROWING UP

The one who plants and the one who waters have
one purpose, and they will each be rewarded
according to their own labor.
1 CORINTHIANS 3:8

Lord, what will be the fruit of my child's life? I pray for your blessing over what they will do with their mind, abilities, and future. Sometimes I worry about what they might do for a vocation in the ever-changing landscape of industry and opportunity. Please help me not to ask "what if," but to remember that whatever they do will have a purpose, and you will know, see, and guide their effort—and their heart—toward that purpose. You call some to plant, some to water, some to prune, and some to reap…but all are a part of the harvest.

Thank you, Lord, for caring about how this child grows up…and how they will grow into the role and purpose you have for them.

PEACE SEEKER, PEACE MAKER

Consider the blameless, observe the upright;
a future awaits those who seek peace.
PSALM 37:37

Lord, I place my hope for my child's future in your hands. I know the goodness you hold for them. When the world feels out of control and the question marks loom large, I turn my focus to you and your Word, and I pray your plans over my child. May they become one who considers the blameless, observes the upright, and seeks peace.

I pray you will give my child the strength of a warrior and the heart of a healer so they stand strong for others. Bless my child with a thirst for mercy and justice. Maybe they will become a leader of peacemakers and build bridges to reunite people and lands that have been divided. With a grateful heart, I will dream of my child's possibilities in you.

INTEGRITY

———————

MAY MY CHILD LIVE AND
TREAT OTHERS WITH HONOR,
WHOLENESS, AND INTEGRITY.

———————

WHOLLY LOVED

You were taught, with regard to your former
way of life, to put off your old self, which is
being corrupted by its deceitful desires; to
be made new in the attitude of your minds;
and to put on the new self, created to be like
God in true righteousness and holiness.
Ephesians 4:22-24

When my child was born, I was head over heels for them from head to toe. Just like that, Lord, I was gladly trading in my old life for a new life with my baby. It was a miracle. It is amazing that you offer such a miracle to each of your children, including the one I held years ago. When my child trades in their old ways of brokenness for the life lived in grace, handle their heart with care. Enable me to inspire them to renew their mind and seek integrity and wholeness in you. It's difficult to consider that they will sometimes be sinking, sinful, and afraid. Thank you for being the Lord who will hold my child and fall in love with them from head to toe.

TROUBLED

---

*Consider it pure joy, my brothers and
sisters, whenever you face trials of many
kinds, because you know that the testing
of your faith produces perseverance.*
JAMES 1:2-3

When it comes to toys, friends, and snacks, my child is eager for variety. Not so much when it comes to trials. Yet over the course of their life, they'll experience an abundance of discomforts and obstacles. Lord, allow each test of my child's faith to be a catalyst for perseverance in and dependence on you. A difficulty that makes them pause to lean into your integrity as the compassionate, Almighty Lord becomes a chance for you to forge their character and their trust in you. Bless my child with spiritual eyes to notice those gifts emerging. And when my worries entice me to smooth the way, may I choose instead to point out your hand at work so hope will carry my child beyond discouragement to joy in all circumstances.

READY TO HEAR IT

Whoever heeds life-giving correction
will be at home among the wise.
Proverbs 15:31

Another round of arguments over my child's misbehavior has left our home divided, tense. The well-intended instruction I offered turned into fodder for a fight. Lord, you see our struggle, and you know our hearts. Give me strength and compassion to stand firm when I approach my child with guidance. Grant my child the sense of being fully loved so they willingly receive your life-giving correction in Scripture and conviction in their spirit.

Give them a foundation of integrity and the ability to live with healthy boundaries and helpful criticism. I thank you today for the leader they can become as they welcome guidance and are at home with the humble and wise.

PERSONAL GUIDE

Good and upright is the LORD;
therefore he instructs sinners in his ways.
He guides the humble in what is right
and teaches them his way.
PSALM 25:8-9

A day will come when my child will be uncertain which way to go. God, let my child be tender and attentive to your will and instruction in your way. A situation will unfold in which they will want to make the right decision but won't be sure what that is. An obstacle might cause them to question who they are and what they are pursuing. Give them ears and a spirit eager to tune in to your personal guidance and the path that leads to your best for them. In those times, shape in them a humble heart that is ready to follow you alone. Lead them into a life of integrity—not because they are without sin, but because they are with you.

HOPE UP AHEAD

We also glory in our sufferings, because
we know that suffering produces perseverance;
perseverance, character; and character, hope.
ROMANS 5:3-4

Jesus, as my child grows into who you designed them to become, I pray you will bless them with glimpses of the light up ahead. Recognizing the importance of integrity in one's youth isn't easy. Distractions and detours are more attractive. Give my child a healthy, hopeful respect for the impact of each decision. When they want to give up on a commitment because it is difficult, show them the power of persevering and keeping their word. If they're tempted to go along with a peer's bad attitude, nudge them to stand firm so they don't regret speaking harmful words. And when discouragement makes them question whether their role matters, let them feel the hope you bring into the world through those who walk in unconditional love, integrity, and godliness.

PORTRAIT OF THE HEART

The LORD said to Samuel, "Do not consider his
appearance or his height, for I have rejected him.
The LORD does not look at the things people look at.
People look at the outward appearance,
but the LORD looks at the heart."
1 SAMUEL 16:7

Lord, teach me about my child. Oh, I know the day-to-day moods. I know the wardrobe choices they use to push boundaries (or my buttons). I'm familiar with the grimace they make for family photos. But you look at their heart. You know its rough edges, its smooth spaces, and its unique potential. I want to notice their heart's capacity for faith, love, and integrity more than I focus on their clothing trends or the roll of their eyes.

Give me a portrait of their heart, Lord, so I can memorize it and reflect it back to them with love. Sure, they might roll their eyes when they hear my words of appreciation, but I don't mind as long as my love sinks into their heart.

STRENGTH AND
CONFIDENCE

MAY MY CHILD TRUST IN YOUR

STRENGTH AND STAND ON IT, LORD.

STRENGTH OF YOUTH

*Command and teach these things. Don't let anyone
look down on you because you are young, but set
an example for the believers in speech, in
conduct, in love, in faith and in purity.*
1 TIMOTHY 4:11-12

Lord, it must grieve you when people seek value and
delight apart from you and your intentions for them.
It doesn't take many birthdays for a little human to
start looking to outside factors to gauge their worth
and to question whether they have anything to offer.
When my child gets stressed about trying to fit in at
school or in other groups, their rumblings of doubt
and self-deprecation break my heart. I don't ever want
my child to shrink from challenges or opportunities to
be themselves.

Lord, bless them with the strength of youth fueled
by your truth. Fill them with bravery to shine, to be set
apart in their speech, life, love, faith, and purity. May
they never feel "less than" for being young and faithful.

CONSTANT COMPANION

*Be strong and courageous. Do not be
afraid or terrified because of them, for
the LORD your God goes with you; he
will never leave you nor forsake you.*
DEUTERONOMY 31:6

Jesus, I want my child to know and believe that you are always with them no matter where they go. As the years go by, they will spend less time with me and with our family. Give them assurance that you are their constant companion. Allow my faith-filled words to ease their worries about what is ahead.

When we hit hard times as a family, let them sense your peaceful presence and see your power at work on our behalf. I'm so grateful that these examples in their youth will inspire their willingness to lean into your strength as they grow into the people you've blessed them to become.

SOMETHING TO OFFER

Each of you has your own gift from God;
one has this gift, another has that.
1 CORINTHIANS 7:7

God, rarely a day goes by that I'm not simultaneously challenged and delighted by my child's attributes and strengths. I'm in awe of this creation before me. My words of gratitude and appreciation for who they are barely begin to reveal the depth of my thankfulness. May they, too, be thankful for how you made them and for the faith and purpose you've given them.

When I point out their abilities and kindness as they solve problems, include others, and put friends' plans ahead of their own, let my words sink in and build their confidence. May my words mingle with the words you impress on their soul so they always believe that they have important gifts to offer and that they themselves are a gift from you to the world.

WHERE MY CHILD STANDS

---

*The LORD upholds all who fall
and lifts up all who are bowed down.*
PSALM 145:14

Lord, I can relax when I rest in the truth that you have my child covered. Give them an abiding belief and a steadfast hope in your presence and support. As they grow, this trust in your might and faithfulness will infuse them with a strength that endures and multiplies when it is tested.

When they fall, you uphold them with mercy and empower them to get up and go forward with renewed conviction. And when they are humble before you, full of questions and, I pray, praises, may you lift them up. They can stand in your presence and feel their confidence grow. And everyone will see that their success and transformation are because of their sure foundation of your strength and love.

PEACE WHERE THERE IS FEAR

When I am afraid, I put my trust in you.
In God, whose word I praise—
in God I trust and am not afraid.
PSALM 56:3-4

God, you have given my child an example to follow when fear billows in, clouding their faith and obscuring their view of the path ahead. You give them access to your heart and guidance the second they put their trust in you for their immediate needs and worries. Steer them toward light when darkness threatens their belief. Hold their hand and accompany them so they have confidence when making friends, starting a new year of school, or expressing their feelings.

As they grow, I won't know which fears will cloud their thoughts, but I'm so grateful that you will see those fears and walk my child through them to your light and clarity, Lord.

WHOM GOD CAN USE

Moses said to the LORD, "Since I speak with
faltering lips, why would Pharaoh listen to me?"
EXODUS 6:30

Lord, anchor in my child a sincere belief that your strength and power flow through them. When you place things on their heart to share with others, please bless them with boldness to express those messages and insights. When they falter in action or speech, help them rely on your courage. It will fuel the confidence they need to lift their voice or move forward.

May my child recognize that as you stir their spirit with words to deliver, you also work in the minds and hearts of those who hear those encouragements. Let them surrender their whole being so they can watch with awe as you use every weakness, mistake, and strength in the making to accomplish great things in your name.

PROVISION

MAY MY CHILD LIVE EVERY DAY

THANKFUL FOR YOUR CARE, LORD.

GOD'S RADAR

The LORD will keep you from all harm—
he will watch over your life; the LORD will
watch over your coming and going
both now and forevermore.
PSALM 121:7-8

God, my parental intuition is quite good. I know when my child is trying to get out of following instructions. I sense when they want to ask me something but are afraid to bring it up. And I know when they've pillaged the snacks. But Lord, none of that compares with your ability to watch over my child. As my child faces difficult seasons, they don't need my intuition and hovering. They need to sense your protective presence and to be grateful for it. May they place their security in you as you watch over their days.

There is nowhere my child can go that is out of your sight and earshot. Thank you for being a loving, protective Abba Father who will forever have my child on his radar and his heart.

GIVING CREDIT

You may say to yourself, "My power and the
strength of my hands have produced this wealth
for me." But remember the LORD your God, for
it is he who gives you the ability to produce
wealth, and so confirms his covenant, which
he swore to your ancestors, as it is today.
DEUTERONOMY 8:17-18

Lord, all things come from your hands. All blessings rise from your mercies and generosity. The goodness that will be a part of my child's future will be your doing. Jesus, in all my child's creativity, work, efforts, and opportunities, I pray they'll know the truth about you and praise your provision. Each time they taste success, spark hope in others, or experience deep joy, please give them the wisdom to give credit to you.

Cultivate in my child a humble spirit that responds with thanksgiving to your faithful care. Give them a readiness, an eagerness to tell others that what they have done, what they have, and who they are—all these things are because of you.

KNOWN

Are not five sparrows sold for two pennies? Yet not one of them is forgotten by God. Indeed, the very hairs of your head are all numbered. Don't be afraid; you are worth more than many sparrows.
LUKE 12:6-7

Dear Jesus, pursue my child. I see their hunger to be known and counted when they are with friends and family. When they don't feel included, they are sad, mopey, discouraged. I can remind them again and again of my love for them, yet I know that even more, they need to know that *you* see and value them. They don't fully recognize this need yet, but they know the longing and ache of not being cared for by those from whom they try to gain acceptance.

Show up in their life as protector and provider. When they feel left out or invisible to others, remind them that you watch over them 24/7. Each time their spirit is boosted by someone, may they receive that warmth and acceptance as a small sign of your love for them.

CALLING ON GOD

———

*Jabez cried out to the God of Israel, "Oh,
that you would bless me and enlarge my
territory! Let your hand be with me, and
keep me from harm so that I will be free
from pain." And God granted his request.*
1 Chronicles 4:10

Lord, you know what's in store for my child. What
they will do with their time, their hands, their mind,
their days. Plant within them the seed of dependence
and anticipation so they immediately turn to you and
call on your name at every turn. May they look forward
to your response of support to expand their life work to
serve you and others.

My hope is that everything they have and are
responsible for will be reminders of your provision. As
you expand my child's influence, protect them phys-
ically and spiritually, God. When hardship intersects
their journey, let them call on you for blessings of healing and continued progress fulfilling their purpose.

PLANTING PLENTY

He will also send you rain for the seed you
sow in the ground, and the food that comes
from the land will be rich and plentiful.
ISAIAH 30:23

Giver of all, establish in my child a deep gratitude for the bounty you provide. We can become so distant from the growing cycle of plants and the life cycle of animals and people that we overlook the miraculous order you've established for the earth and your creations. It provides beginnings, harvests, times of rest, necessary endings, and rebirth.

Lord, I believe this is true of spiritual cycles as well. Let your provision rain down so the seeds of purpose will sprout and take root. Protect my child from shallow pursuits that drain their energy and hope and produce nothing. Plant in them what you long to see harvested. May they produce rich and plentiful blessings they can offer back to you with delight and awe.

THIS LAND IS YOUR LAND

---

*Walk in obedience to all that the LORD your God
has commanded you, so that you may
live and prosper and prolong your days
in the land that you will possess.*
DEUTERONOMY 5:33

Every place my child will walk, visit, fly over, hike through, or savor the view of is part of your grand creation, Lord. I pray my child will have a sense of stewardship and responsibility when it comes to your land, including the terrain of their faith journey. May every step be on the path you carve for them. Their life won't necessarily be easy, but it can be godly. Stir in my child a deep reverence for your will so they serve the places and people you lead them to…whether it's a quiet suburban home, a growing church, a Bible study group, a blended family, or a studio apartment in a bustling city.

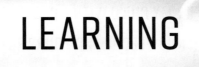

LEARNING

FILL MY CHILD WITH A PASSION
FOR KNOWLEDGE AND YOUR TRUTH.

LEARNED APPRECIATION

Since my youth, God, you have taught me,
and to this day I declare your marvelous deeds.
PSALM 71:17

The discussions in our home are often about homework. Where is it? What is it? Did you get it done? God, you see this conversation play out every week during the school year. I'm trying to provide my child with resources and encouragement to grow in knowledge. I don't expect them to declare their appreciation for this effort now or in their later days. However, I hope my child will one day express their gratitude for all *you* have taught them. And if they do learn anything directly from me, let it be to praise you for your marvelous deeds and to honor you at every age by living out the wisdom you pour into the hearts of your children.

TEACHING HOPE

I am a friend to all who fear you,
to all who follow your precepts.
The earth is filled with your love, LORD;
teach me your decrees.
PSALM 119:63-64

Jesus, help me shift my language and my emphasis when talking to my child about life. When I am about to ramble on about the risks and potential pitfalls around every corner, or when I'm seconds from warning them about stranger danger for the umpteenth time, hold me back. Fill me with the love and wonder my child needs to learn about. This world, this earth, and our lives are filled with so much beauty and goodness. Let the only fear we dwell on be a healthy fear of you and your might.

Yes, I want my child to be prepared to make smart, safe choices. But much more, I want their heart to absorb the instruction in your decrees that produces a life of hope.

WHOLEHEARTED

Teach me your way, Lord,
that I may rely on your faithfulness;
give me an undivided heart,
that I may fear your name.
Psalm 86:11

Set the course for my child's spiritual learning, dear God. I pray they will walk in your way, your light, and your truth. They will learn many lessons in everyday life, yet everything they discover can be examined through the lens of belief and faithfulness. Give them curiosity so they are industrious and resourceful.

Lord, let your words enter their mind and spirit with ease so they know your voice and heed your wisdom. I pray that they won't ever dismiss what they learn in faith, but that they will be righteous in their pursuit of knowledge of the Spirit. I admire their unabashed love for you and instinct to ask questions about you and the world you made. They teach me daily about living wholehearted for you. I'm forever grateful.

HUMBLE BEGINNINGS

When pride comes, then comes disgrace,
but with humility comes wisdom.
PROVERBS 11:2

Lord, my child is getting too big for their britches. I worry their pride will lead to a big fall. I'm torn between wanting you to protect them from their folly and wanting you to fast-forward to when they realize they have a lot to learn.

I praise you for being with them even when they're challenging. You see their insecurities and know the fears they lift in prayer. God, if these fuel their need to act tough or all-knowing, fill them with your confidence so they can become gentle, patient, and intentional without hurting others. If they are overbearing because they think they succeed in their own power and not yours, then Lord, give them a safe place to land when they fall. May they get back up, seek your wisdom, and begin again with a humble heart.

THIRSTY

Let my teaching fall like rain
and my words descend like dew,
like showers on new grass,
like abundant rain on tender plants.
DEUTERONOMY 32:2

My child is a new expression of life on this earth, Lord. Every cell, every smile, every laugh, every physical and spiritual attribute is freshly formed by you. Each time I see the world reflected in their words or actions, Lord, I worry they will lose the shimmer and openness of youth. I pray they remain a tender being who is thirsty for your words. Your teachings will sustain them and refresh their mind, body, and spirit.

When their daily terrain is marked by discouragement and becomes arid and stifling, may they turn their face upward to receive your knowledge and love, which you shower upon them. In your mercy, Lord, renew their hope in and affection for you, the one who makes the rain and who made them with love and for a purpose.

PURSUE WITH JOY

Flee the evil desires of youth and pursue
righteousness, faith, love and peace, along with
those who call on the Lord out of a pure heart.
2 TIMOTHY 2:22

I can't see my child's future; however, I do know they will stumble. Wrong turns will happen. Mistakes will be made. Doubts will rise. I also know that you will be there with them, Lord. When my child doesn't know where to turn, please reach for their hand and guide them toward righteousness, faith, love, and peace. Connect them to those who have a heart for you and who are both passionate and compassionate in their search for understanding.

Encourage my child to ask questions of peers, leaders, and teachers so they gather knowledge and become empowered, emboldened to use their gifts and experience. God, I pray life's twists and turns ultimately lead them to pursue you with joy and to forever be your hands and heart in this world.

GENEROSITY

MAY MY CHILD SERVE, GIVE,
AND LOVE FROM A SENSE OF
YOUR ABUNDANCE, LORD.

OVERFLOW

In the midst of a very severe trial,
their overflowing joy and their extreme
poverty welled up in rich generosity.
2 CORINTHIANS 8:2

Jesus, you lift us up above our circumstances with your power and grace. I pray that after my child goes through trials, they will come out the other side with a joy that is deep and replenished by your unconditional, unlimited love. May their hope be unbound and unlimited. Allow my child's heart to expand so it becomes a well of generosity to draw from.

I have watched them make it through a rough day and settle into their bedtime prayer with a willingness to begin again…to believe in a second chance, not only for themselves but also for others in need. This fills my spirit with gratitude and awe. They seem to have been born knowing that you make all things new and that you give to us so we can give to others.

FEEL THE LOVE

A new command I give you: Love one another.
As I have loved you, so you must love one another.
By this everyone will know that you are
my disciples, if you love one another.
JOHN 13:34-35

Cover and immerse my child in your love, Jesus. Let their spirit and heart be drenched in your affection. This is how their life of generosity, kindness, compassion, and love will begin. Your unconditional love will inspire their heart and inform their actions to share that love with others. Help me encourage them when they reach out to a hurting classmate or family member with empathy.

Grow in them an unwavering compassion for strangers and those facing injustice or times of hardship. May my child gaze upon other people with your eyes, filled with tenderness. Their motives as a child are innocent and righteous. I pray you will preserve that goodness and godliness as they become an expression of your love in the world.

NO STRINGS ATTACHED

Do nothing out of selfish ambition or vain conceit.
Rather, in humility value others above yourselves.
PHILIPPIANS 2:3

My day is made when my child's deep kindness takes me by surprise. When I see them give in a way that I know is a sacrifice of their own want and comfort, my heart rejoices. As they grow, Lord, expand that ability and capacity to put others above themselves. Build in them a confidence that comes from knowing you and being known by you so they don't make choices to get applause or approval from others. Let them be that rare creature who gives without strings attached or the need for reciprocation.

May they move through their childhood and adulthood with godly confidence. Help them recognize that they want for nothing, so they can give everything—never afraid or selfish, but always filled with pure joy.

LOVE IS

Love is patient, love is kind. It does not envy,
it does not boast, it is not proud. It does not
dishonor others, it is not self-seeking, it is not
easily angered, it keeps no record of wrongs.
1 CORINTHIANS 13:4-5

Father, may our family embrace a 1 Corinthians 13 heart so our actions show what love is and what it can be. I want my child to have this healthy and godly definition of how to honor, serve, and lift up others.

May we be patient, kind, and humble in spirit. May we not be jealous or stingy when it comes to expressing delight and pride in others. The world's love has limits and conditions. It can be self-serving. Bless my child with the spiritual discernment to know the difference. Not only so they will be able to give inspired love to others, but also so they can receive it and know it is pure in intention. I pray for my child to love and be loved with a generosity that comes only from such a giving God.

NEW CREATION

I will give you a new heart and put a new spirit in
you; I will remove from you your heart of stone
and give you a heart of flesh.
EZEKIEL 36:26

There may come a day, Lord, when my child's heart is hardened by life experiences and loss. They will sometimes be truly heartsick and need your healing. Show me if this happens while they are young so I can be a prayerful support as they seek your mercy. And if this happens when they are older, dear Jesus, please lead their weary spirit straight to your presence. That is where a child of God can swap a heart of stone for one of flesh, love, compassion, warmth, kindness, generosity, and grace. It is where my child can discover what it is to live as a new creation in Christ. Once they do, may they realize they wouldn't trade this new life for anything the world has to offer!

EXCELLENT GIVER

Since you excel in everything—in faith, in speech,
in knowledge, in complete earnestness and in
the love we have kindled in you—see that
you also excel in this grace of giving.
2 CORINTHIANS 8:7

praise you for having open arms, ready to hold my child and transform them from the inside out. Lord, create in my child a sincere faith that seeks your wisdom and is evident in kindness. We measure my child's growth in many ways…from having them stand against the wall to compare their height to the year before, to helping them prepare for life's assignments and challenges. But Lord, the area I want my child to excel in is their ability to give. May their generosity never be limited by hesitation, doubt, or the imposed boundaries on what they offer a stranger, a friend…you. Maybe next year, instead of measuring their height, we can celebrate the depth of their giving heart.

GRATITUDE

MAY MY CHILD'S HEART OVERFLOW
WITH THANKSGIVING
FOR ALL YOU DO AND ARE, LORD.

BEST GIFT EVER

I will give them a heart to know me, that I am the
LORD. They will be my people, and I will be their
God, for they will return to me with all their heart.
JEREMIAH 24:7

In my child's youth, they are learning and growing. I pray they will always eagerly and earnestly desire to understand you. May they know you as Lord when they are afraid. May they embrace you as Shepherd when they are lost. May they call on you as Redeemer when they fall. And however they reach out, I pray it will be with gratitude for the gift of being your child.

I see them now enjoying the treasures of knowing you as Lord—peace, confidence, assurance. They don't complicate those gifts like I do; they simply believe. It fills me with joy because I know these early days of faith will create a path they can always follow to you with a full and grateful heart.

THERE IS A REASON

My dear brothers and sisters, stand firm.
Let nothing move you. Always give yourselves
fully to the work of the Lord, because you know
that your labor in the Lord is not in vain.
1 Corinthians 15:58

Lord, help me train my child to have a strong character, faith, and sense of compassion for others. I want them to be able to stand firm in their love for you as they commit to the work you give them. Even at this age, they can express their faith by being a good friend, offering encouragement, and honoring their word.

Don't let them equate stubbornness with standing firm, Lord. Guide them toward a steadfastness that serves you so when life challenges them or they don't get the result they want, they are still grateful to you. There is a reason for their efforts. Nothing is done in vain, because their Abba Father is making use of all things.

OPPORTUNITIES TO GIVE THANKS

Be joyful in hope, patient in affliction,
faithful in prayer. Share with the
Lord's people who are in need.
ROMANS 12:12-13

Be joyful! I want to encourage and inspire my child toward this every day. Lord, place in them an eternal light that illumines the hope and possibility of every moment, trouble, need to pray, and time of waiting and wondering. Fill them with a sense of awe as they realize that every act of giving can be a reason to be joyful and grateful. Each new morning is an opportunity to appreciate the life they are given.

As a family, may we celebrate more than we deliberate over whether something is good or not good. Save us from wasting time when there are endless ways to be lights in the world and to share your love with others.

WAIT FOR IT

You wearied yourself by such going about,
but you would not say, "It is hopeless."
You found renewal of your strength,
and so you did not faint.
ISAIAH 57:10

If my child becomes discouraged working on a task or plodding through the daily routine, Lord, help them to trust you for refreshment and to remember to be thankful. Inspire them with hope when they need it. I truly believe that when they are weary and weak, they will discover your power to restore.

Life is filled with energy-draining distractions and dilemmas. But each encounter with a challenge can lead them to grow and to trust you. Empower my child to leap over a first response to give up and instead to give their every need to you. May their grateful heart anticipate and receive the renewal you promise and the strength to press on.

IN YOUR SIGHT

Whoever lives by the truth comes into the light,
so that it may be seen plainly that what they
have done has been done in the sight of God.
JOHN 3:21

Jesus, walk with my child. Guard them from taking things for granted. I want them to count and treasure the blessings that come from your hand. I pray they will live by your truth and express their faith openly so others can witness their gratitude for you and recognize that it is sincere. Give my child a spirit that is quick to be thankful for the gifts of new days, new friends, new knowledge. May my child reflect your light in the world. I love seeing how they already want to bring their dreams, hurts, and hopes to you right away. They aren't holding back any part of themselves, even when they stumble. I am deeply grateful that they will live their entire journey in your sight. May what you see bring joy to your heart, dear Lord.

ONE DAY AT A TIME

Do not boast about tomorrow,
for you do not know what a day may bring.
PROVERBS 27:1

My child is learning that today's opportunities and challenges will change as their tomorrows unfold. God, help me to teach them the importance of the present moment and to give them a healthy respect for all they don't know. I want them to have confidence without arrogance. And I pray their confidence will be in you and not in their own desires or plans.

My deepest hope is for them to wake up each day with gratitude and a willingness to surrender that day to you. This is such an adult lesson. Give me the words to speak into their life, Lord. I cannot tell them what each day will bring, but I can confidently tell them who walks with them and guides them each day. Thank you, Jesus.

ABOUT THE AUTHORS

Michelle Lind is a pastor's wife, a teacher, and a mother to a blended group of five amazing kids. Michelle loves music, teaching, traveling, and writing. She grew up in the church and is actively involved in her church now. Michelle is a graduate of Bushnell University (BA) and the University of Oregon (MS). Enjoy her writing and insights on her blog at lifeinaglassbowl.com.

Hope Lyda is an editor, trained spiritual director, praying auntie, and author whose books have sold more than one million copies. She has published more than 35 titles, including *One-Minute Prayers® for Women, One-Minute Prayers® for Moms, My Unedited Writing Year, Life as a Prayer,* and *What Do You Need Today?* Follow Hope at @mywritedirection or visit her at www.mywritedirection.com.

OTHER PRAYER BOOKS YOU MIGHT ENJOY

From Hope Lyda...

One-Minute Prayers® for Moms

One-Minute Prayers® for a Woman's Year

One-Minute Prayers® to Start Your Day

One-Minute Prayers® for Women

One-Minute Prayers® for Wives

From other writers...

One-Minute Prayers® for Dads
NICK HARRISON

Prayers for Parents of Prodigals
LINDA S. CLARE

Raise Them Up: Praying God's Word over Your Kids
SALLY BURKE AND CINDY CLAYPOOL DE NEVE

The Power of a Praying® Mom
STORMIE OMARTIAN